body story

SPREADING MENACE

Salmonella Attack
and
The Hunger Craving

BLACKBIRCH®
PRESS

THOMSON
★
GALE

San Diego • Detroit • New York • San Francisco • Cleveland • New Haven, Conn. • Waterville, Maine • London • Munich

THOMSON

GALE

LIBRARY OF CONGRESS CATALOGING-IN-PUBLICATION DATA

Spreading menace / Elaine Pascoe, book editor.
   p. cm. — (Body story)
Summary: Describes the effects of salmonella, a type of food poisoning, on a photographer who ate undercooked chicken the day before shooting a calendar for a frozen food company.
Includes bibliographical references and index.
  ISBN 1-4103-0064-1 (hdbk. : alk. paper) — ISBN 1-4103-0185-0 (pbk. : alk. paper)
  1. Salmonella—Juvenile literature. 2. Salmonellosis—Juvenile literature. [1. Salmonella. 2. Food poisoning. 3. Diseases.] I. Pascoe, Elaine. II. Series.

QR201.S25S67 2004
615.9'529344—dc21
                                             2003009641

Printed in China
10 9 8 7 6 5 4 3 2 1

SALMONELLA ATTACK

This chicken is hiding a deadly secret.

Its intestines are a breeding ground. They are riddled with salmonella bacteria.

The salmonella do nothing to harm the chicken. They live in peaceful coexistence with their host. But salmonella are always looking to invade other animals.

Top: Salmonella makes its home in the intestines of chickens.

Bottom: Salmonella do not harm the chicken, but are always on the hunt for a new host.

And when they do, it's a different story—as photographer Mike Small is about to find out.

It's going to be a big week for Mike. He's taken on a last-minute assignment, shooting a calendar for a frozen food company. The company chief, Kathleen O'Marn, needs the twelve photos—one for each month, featuring a different employee and a different product—by the end of the week.

Top: Photographer Mike Small has no idea what the next week will be like.

Bottom: Mike's client, Kathleen, wants him to create a calendar for her frozen food company.

While Mike finishes up in the studio, Mary, his wife, is preparing dinner. She's unaware that, even though the chicken she's preparing is dead, it is still seething with life. Deep inside, its flesh is crawling with millions of salmonella bacteria.

But if the salmonella are going to survive, they need a new living host.

Top: Mary, Mike's wife, does not know how many bacteria live in the chicken she is preparing.

Bottom: The salmonella bacteria in the chicken need to find a living host.

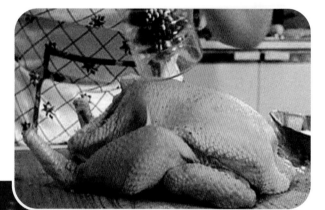

Even though the chicken has been cooked, thousands of salmonella still thrive inside.

DEADLY INVASION

In the oven, the salmonella bacteria closest to the surface of the chicken are roasted alive. None survive in the chicken's breast. But the flesh around the leg bones is undercooked. Here the temperature fails to reach 158 degrees Fahrenheit (70 degrees Celsius), and hundreds of thousands of salmonella are still alive.

As he begins to eat, Mike Small is unaware that he's about to play host to uninvited guests. One gulp carries thousands of salmonella into his stomach. There they are promptly attacked by digestive acids. But, unfortunately for Mike, a few of the bacteria survive the acid bath. Now they are swept down into his intestines by the muscular contractions that are part of the process of digestion.

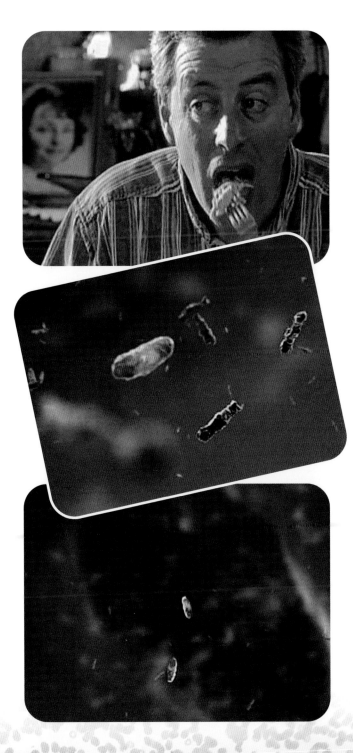

Top: Mike is unaware of the danger while he eats his dinner.

Middle: Microscopic salmonella sweep into Mike's stomach as he eats.

Bottom: Some bacteria survive the digestive acids in Mike's stomach.

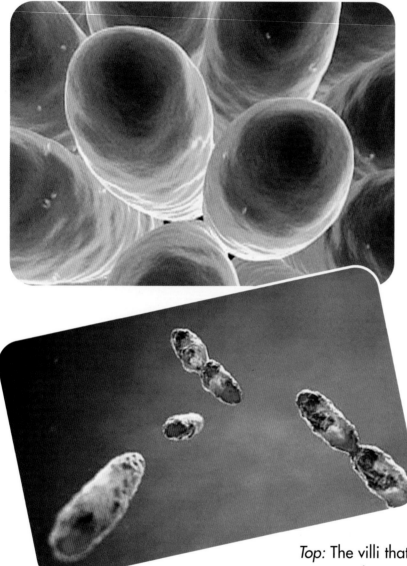

The salmonella bacteria need a safe place to multiply. They drift toward the lining of Mike's gut, where fingerlike projections, called villi, absorb water and nutrients. The salmonella head for the cells on the villi surface. The moment they land, they invade these cells and start to multiply.

Top: The villi that line Mike's gut absorb water and nutrients, and now ... salmonella.

Bottom: The salmonella begin to multiply as soon as they land on the villi.

Now that they have a foothold in Mike's gut, the salmonella bacteria will do two things: breed and spread. Only two hours after the cells lining his intestine were first invaded, the infected cells begin to die. The salmonella burst out of the cells they've destroyed. They spread to neighboring cells, infect them, and begin the whole process again.

Within eight hours, there are a million salmonella bacteria in Mike's gut. In another hour, there will be 4 million of these deadly invaders.

Top: Intestine cells die just two hours after salmonella infect them.

Middle: Salmonella spread and breed immediately.

Bottom: Nine hours later, 4 million salmonella have invaded Mike's gut.

THE BODY'S DEFENSE

Mike's body needs to defend itself. And while he may not be aware of the salmonella attack, his body is already reacting to it.

As cells die, they release a chemical distress signal that alerts Mike's immune system to the invasion and calls in a rapid-reaction force—mobile defense cells called macrophages. These cells capture the invaders and release a deadly cocktail of poisons to destroy them.

Top: While Mike sleeps, his body starts to react to the bacteria and defend against it.

Bottom: Microphages of the immune system attack the invasive bacteria.

But the salmonella have a secret weapon, a chemical counterdefense that disables the macrophages. Now the bacteria can breed untouched, even invading and multiplying inside the macrophages that were sent to destroy them.

At his studio the next day, Mike meets with Kathleen O'Marn to begin the calendar photo shoot. The salmonella have been breeding for more than twelve hours at this point, and as yet Mike feels no symptoms. But all that is about to change.

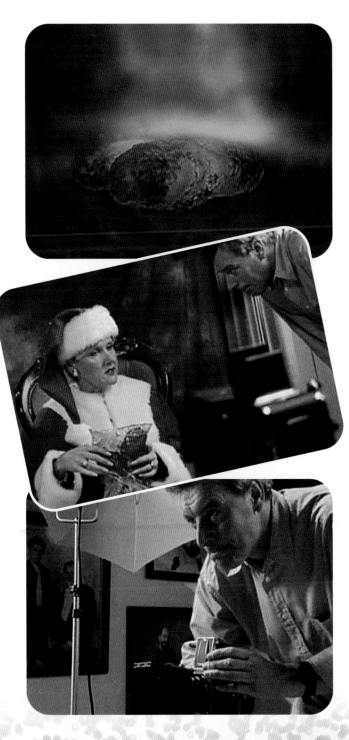

Top: The bacteria resist the chemical attack of the defensive cells and continue to breed.

Middle: Mike and Kathleen work together on the photo shoot.

Bottom: Mike still feels fine, despite the millions of salmonella that multiply inside his body.

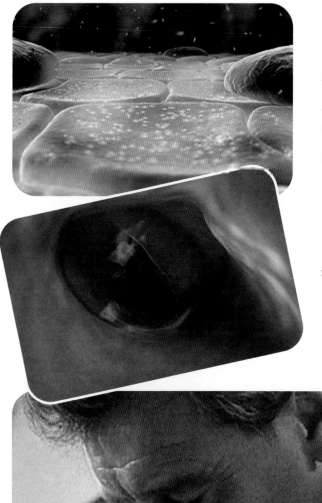

Top: The salmonella continue to destroy Mike's cells.

Middle: Mike's digestive system begins to react to the bacteria.

Bottom: Mike starts to feel nauseated.

With his macrophages out of action, his body has to resort to cruder methods for dealing with the salmonella. As the bacteria destroy more and more cells, the chemical distress signals in his body reach a critical level and trigger a physical reaction in Mike's digestive system. The contractions switch into reverse in an attempt to expel the salmonella bacteria.

Mike begins to feel nauseous. His body prepares for a violent expulsion. Food shoots from his intestine back into his stomach and up his esophagus. The flap to his windpipe slams shut. Another blocks off his nose, and he vomits. That brings the photo session to a fast close, and Mike goes home. For the first time, he's aware of the invasion in his body.

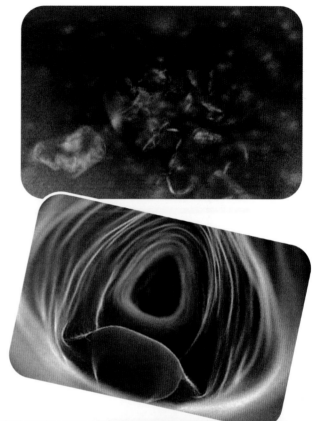

Top: Food from Mike's intestines shoots into his stomach.

Middle: The flaps to Mike's windpipe and nose close.

Bottom: When Mike vomits, he finally realizes something is wrong in his body.

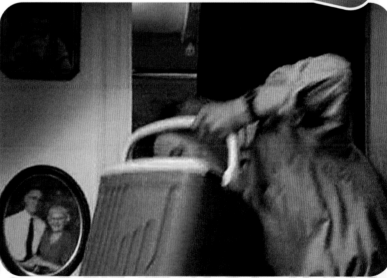

Top: Bacteria still swarm deep in Mike's intestines and vomiting cannot expel the invaders.

Bottom: The discomfort Mike feels is low in his gut, where fluid has built up.

But vomiting has cleared only the top few inches of Mike's intestine. Most of the salmonella bacteria are much farther down. Instead of reversing direction, the contractions farther down in his intestines accelerate. Fluid rushes through faster than Mike's ravaged gut can absorb it. And it's all gathering at the bottom of his intestines. An unmistakable sensation is building in his bowels. Usually Mike can override this urge. But fluid is building up so fast that he is about to lose all control.

Diarrhea may be unpleasant, but it's actually helping Mike fight the bacteria. A single bout flushes around 5 million salmonella from his intestines. Right now this is his body's only hope of slowing down the spread of the bacteria.

Top: Diarrhea helps the body fight salmonella.

Bottom: Mike's body works to slow the bacteria's spread.

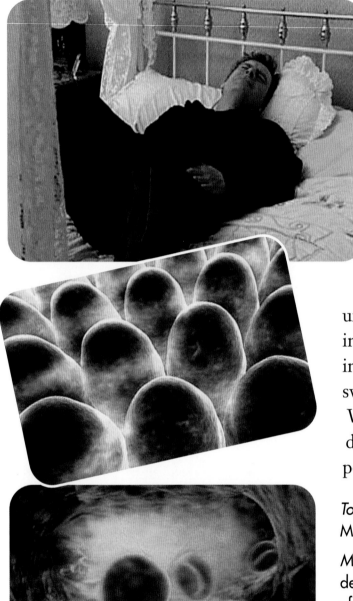

DAY TWO

Mike has been suffering the torments of the salmonella invasion for twenty-four hours. Losing control of his bowels is only one of his problems. The fierce contractions of his gut are causing severe cramps. And as more cells are destroyed, the chemicals they release are building up, with unpleasant side effects. They leak into Mike's bloodstream and seep into his muscles, making them swell. Mike's entire body aches. What's more, the diarrhea is dehydrating him, giving him a pounding headache.

Top: On the second day of his infection, Mike suffers from severe cramps.

Middle: Chemicals released from destroyed cells cause painful side effects.

Bottom: The chemicals have moved through Mike's bloodstream to his muscles and make them swell.

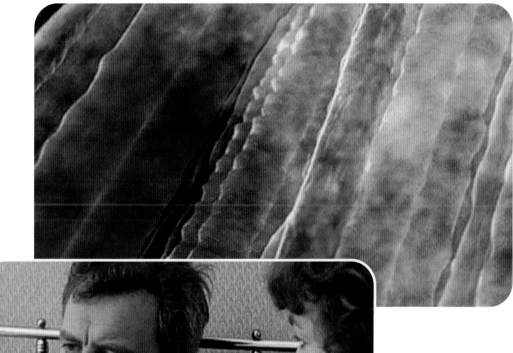

Top: The swelling of Mike's muscles makes his entire body ache.

Above: Mike and Mary realize that the chicken caused Mike's discomfort.

Mike and Mary suspect that the chicken, a half-price special from Ben's Hens, made him sick. But Mike's biggest worry now is his work. He had lined up a full morning of photo sessions for the calendar, and he fears he'll lose the job if he reschedules.

To get through the day ahead, Mike needs help. He turns to medication. Diarrhea pills contain chemicals that slow down the contractions in his gut, returning them to their normal speed. The pills relieve the worst of Mike's symptoms and allow him to work, but they're just a quick fix.

In a way, taking diarrhea pills is a mistake for Mike. Without his macrophages, Mike's body has been fighting a losing battle.

Top: Medication can help slow down Mike's diarrhea.

Middle: Diarrhea pills return the stomach's contractions to a normal speed.

Bottom: The pills only help temporarily.

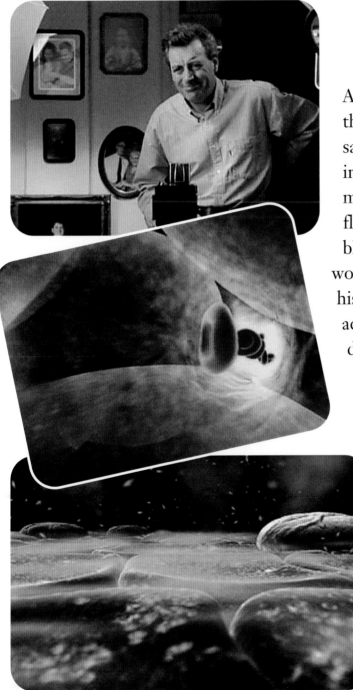

And now, without diarrhea, there's nothing to hold the salmonella back. As the invasion picks up pace, more distress chemicals flood into Mike's bloodstream. His aches are worse than ever. Mike needs his immune system back in action if he is going to defeat the bacteria.

Top: As more chemicals flow into the bloodstream, Mike's aches get worse.

Middle: The pills have stopped the diarrhea, but now the salmonella can spread again.

Bottom: With his immune system down, Mike cannot fight the bacteria.

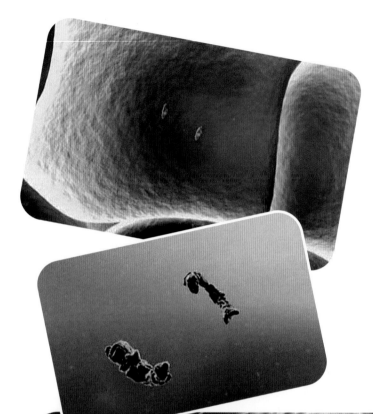

TURNING POINT

As the salmonella spread, a secondary defense system is about to be triggered. Mike's body mobilizes specialized scavenger cells. To the invading salmonella, these cells appear to be like any other cells—but they actually work as traps. Once infected by salmonella bacteria, a scavenger cell neutralizes the invader and passes it into a lymph gland.

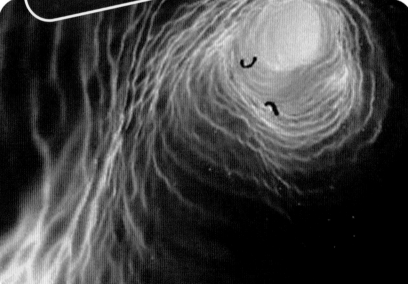

Top: Cells that work as part of a secondary defense system trap the salmonella.

Middle: Scavenger cells neutralize the invading bacteria.

Bottom: The neutralized salmonella pass into the lymph gland.

Within the gland, the bacteria come into contact with helper cells, another part of the immune system. The arrival of the salmonella triggers helper cells that recognize this specific threat to multiply and flood out of the gland. But their target isn't the salmonella. It's the inactive macrophages.

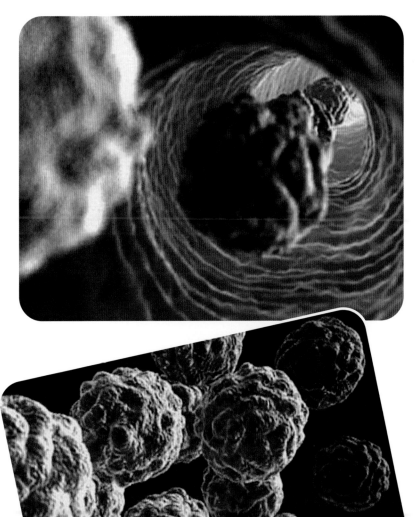

Top: Salmonella trigger helper cells in the lymph gland.

Bottom: Helper cells stream from the lymph gland on a search for macrophages.

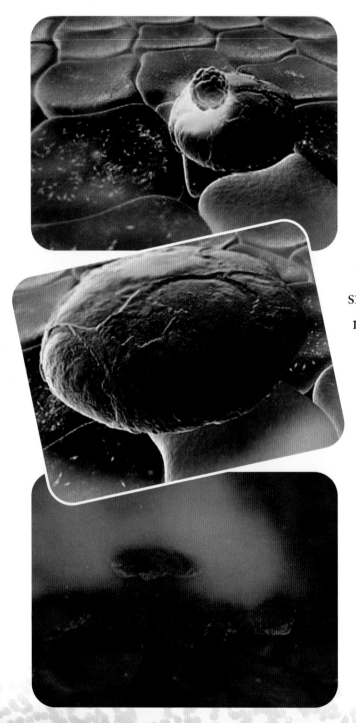

The helper cells release a chemical stimulant that triggers a remarkable metamorphosis. It transforms the macrophages from useless bacteria-infested cells into vicious killers. They double in size, and they become faster and more efficient. They are able to pump out their salmonella-killing poisons so rapidly that the bacteria are helpless. Their advance through the body is halted.

Top: Helper cells release chemicals that cure the inactive macrophages.

Middle: The macrophages are out for revenge on the salmonella.

Bottom: The microphages emit strong poisons that effectively kill the bacteria.

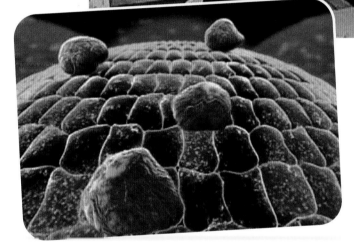

At last the battle is turning in Mike's favor. His symptoms quickly fade—and he finishes the calendar on schedule.

It will take a few weeks to clear out the millions of salmonella bacteria that have colonized Mike's gut, but his victory is assured. People who are very young, old, or have weak immune systems often face greater danger from salmonella. But Mike, like most people with healthy immune systems, was able to defeat the bacterial invasion.

Top: Mike's body has overcome the bacteria and he is able to return to work.

Bottom: Because of his healthy immune system, Mike defeated salmonella.

Top: Chicken are unwitting carriers of salmonella.

Bottom: Salmonella live on, constantly in search of new hosts.

As for the salmonella, they have lost one battle. But as long as they have carriers, they'll be around to fight another day.

THE HUNGER CRAVING

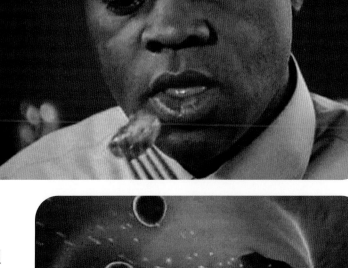

George Frasier is filling up with fuel.

His stomach is a refinery, separating the raw materials from his lunch and passing them into his gut. And there is one form of fuel his body craves above all others, a fuel that is absorbed

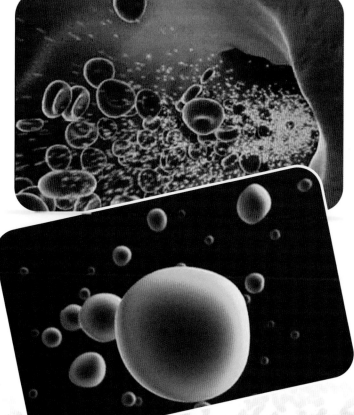

Top: George eats to fuel his body with energy.

Middle: The stomach identifies raw materials and passes them through the gut.

Bottom: The body craves fat molecules more than any other fuel.

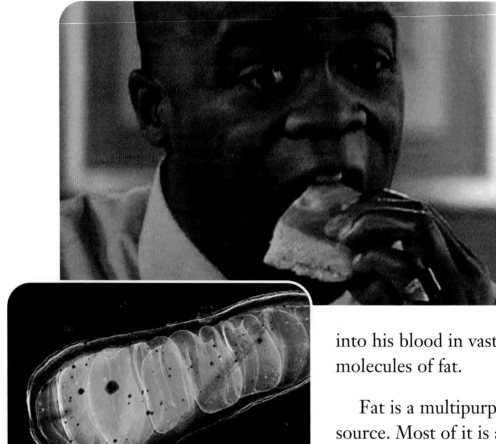

into his blood in vast quantities: molecules of fat.

Fat is a multipurpose fuel source. Most of it is absorbed by cells. Inside the cells, it is drawn toward structures called mitochondria, which are the power generators of the body. Here the fat is burned, releasing the energy that drives life.

But what George's body really wants is a surplus of fat. In fact, his body will even turn nonfatty foods,

Top: The body can turn nonfatty foods from protein to fat.

Bottom: Cell structures, called mitochondria, burn fat.

such as carbohydrates from potatoes and pasta or proteins from meat, into fat if he eats them to excess.

And George is eating to excess. This is just a weekday lunch with business associates—one of whom, Lorraine Harper, he's attracted to. But even before George starts on the cheese selection that's the final course of his meal, he has eaten far more food than his body needs. His blood is awash with more fat than his mitochondria can burn.

Top: George and Lorraine enjoy lunch, but George is eating too much.

Bottom: Now George has more fat in his bloodstream than the mitochondria can burn.

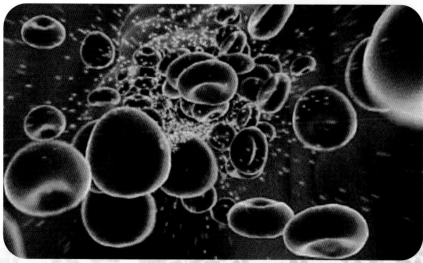

George's growing gut is not just the result of overeating. He shuns exercise, which could increase the amount of fuel his body cells use. He kids Lorraine for planning to work out at the gym that night, suggesting she join him at a club instead. And rather than walking back to his office after lunch, he takes a taxi.

Top: George asks Lorraine to meet him at a nightclub instead of at her gym, where he could burn off fat.

Bottom: If George walked back to his office, his body cells would use more fuel.

FAT AND FAMINE

Fat has real value to George's body. It's the only form of energy that the body can store in vast quantities. Specialized cells absorb fat out of the blood and swell. And as long there is an excess of fat, they will keep growing.

Our craving for fat began in our distant past. Fat stores were good news for our ancestors. They never knew where their next meal was coming from, so having an ample store of fat was good insurance against hard times. But George knows exactly when his next meal is coming. It's rarely more than a few hours away. His fat stores never get depleted. They just grow.

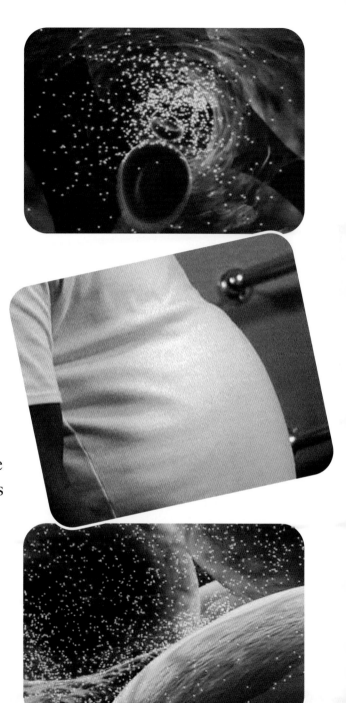

Top: George's body stores large quantities of fat.

Middle: His fat stores never diminish because George eats constantly.

Bottom: Fat stores grow as long as there is an excess of fat.

Top: Women are designed to carry a higher percentage of body fat.

Bottom: Lorraine and George dance at the club; this is George's sole exercise.

On average men have 30 percent less body fat than women. But women are better designed to carry it. They store it mainly on their breasts and hips, giving them vital energy reserves that will see them through the rigors of pregnancy. So although Lorraine weighs seventy pounds less than George does, she has the same amount of body fat.

George is delighted when, as he had hoped, Lorraine joins him and his friends Samson and Jacey at the club that night. It turns out that Lorraine and Jacey know each other—they both go to the same gym.

Lorraine's regular workouts keep her in shape.

George's only exercise is occasional dancing—"Why pump iron when you can shuffle shoe leather?" he says. But shaking his hips once every couple of weeks has little impact on his expanding waistline, and now he's about to discover one of the downsides of his growing fat stores.

When Jacey takes Lorraine aside to quiz her on her interest in George, she gets this reply: "He's really a nice guy, but he's just a bit too overwhelming." It's her way of saying that George's excess weight makes him unattractive to her.

Top: Lorraine is in good shape because she works out on a regular basis.

Bottom: George is crushed that Lorraine is not attracted to him because of his weight.

CRASH DIET

George takes action: He decides to diet his extra weight away. But going on a diet is like volunteering for famine. And George's body is not going to surrender its fat stores without a battle.

Top: George decides to go on a diet and get rid of his excess weight.

Bottom: George throws away all of his junk food in preparation for his diet.

In his war on fat, George is up against a formidable opponent: his own brain. It has been programmed by years of habit to recognize that one o'clock is lunchtime. The right cue—such as a call from a sandwich vendor—sets off a chain reaction of signals that trigger a growing sensation of hunger. Hunger takes hold of George's body. His stomach starts to squeeze what's left of breakfast out of the way, to make space for lunch.

Top: George's brain is programmed to recognize that it is time for lunch.

Middle: Hunger takes over George's body.

Bottom: George's stomach squeezes breakfast aside to make room for lunch.

Top: George decides to have a low-fat tuna sandwich for lunch.

Bottom: The stomach walls can detect a skimpy meal that comes through.

George's intentions are good. He passes up high-fat offerings like salami and Brie cheese, and high-calorie treats like muffins, in favor of plain tuna. But as soon as George looks at his food, his brain starts to calculate how filling it's likely to be. It wants more than just a meal. It wants a satisfying meal. The walls of his stomach contain stretch receptors that estimate the volume of food coming in, confirming the meagerness of this lunch.

George has failed to satisfy his hunger. His body faces an unprecedented situation. He hasn't eaten enough to keep him going, and he needs extra fuel. But his body doesn't turn to his fat stores first. It calls on another kind of fuel—emergency, short-term reserves of glucose, stored in his liver. Glucose molecules are speedy energy boosters. They are released fast and quickly burned in the mitochondria. But they only produce half the energy of fat.

Top: George's body needs more fuel to keep him on the go.

Middle: The body will survive on glucose before it turns to fat stores.

Bottom: Glucose molecules work quickly but do not produce energy that lasts.

George's body would normally top up its glucose stores after every meal. But after four days of dieting, George has eaten so little that his glucose stores are running low. And using up these stores of glucose is having a deceptive effect on his weight loss.

When glucose is stored, large amounts of water are locked up with it. As the glucose is released, so is that water. George is urinating an extra liter a day —and that's a lot of weight. In only four days of dieting, George has lost seven pounds. He's thrilled, but he doesn't realize that almost all of that weight was glucose and water. His stores of body fat are still intact.

His glucose stores, on the other hand, have almost run dry. And when they do, the battle with his body will really begin.

Top and middle: George seems to be losing weight, but his glucose stores are running very low.

Bottom: Most of the weight George has lost has been glucose and water, not fat.

THE BODY FIGHTS BACK

George has managed to resist his hunger drives for a week. He has banished anything fattening from his life. But now his glucose stores are at an all-time low, and to his body this can mean only one thing—famine. There's no choice but to surrender the precious fat reserves back into the bloodstream.

Top: George gets hungry as his glucose stores dwindle.

Bottom: Fat reserves rush back into the bloodstream in an effort to keep hunger at bay.

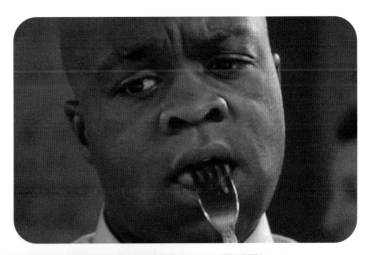

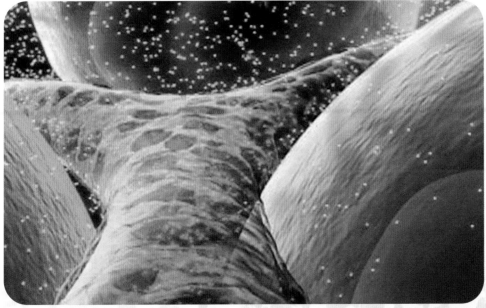

But there's a price to pay. George's fat cells send a warning signal to his brain, which drives his hunger to new extremes. All thoughts are overwhelmed by the aching desire for food. George's hunger drives are interfering with his ability to concentrate on even the simplest of tasks.

His body's reaction sabotages George's diet in another way. Fat stores are being drained, but for survival his body needs to make them last as long as possible. So his body imposes a drastic energy cut. The mitochondria inside his cells start to burn less and less fuel. George is slowing down.

Top and middle: George becomes so hungry that he cannot focus on his work. His brain signals that food is his most important concern.

Bottom: Mitochondria burn fuel more slowly to make the precious fat stores last.

Top: George receives his first disappointment when he finds out that Lorraine has a boyfriend.

Bottom: George's next shock is that his weight loss is at a standstill.

On top of that comes the news that Lorraine Harper already has a boyfriend. George is still convinced that Lorraine could like him—if only she knew the thinner, inner George he knows he could be. But he's in for another disappointment when he checks his weight.

George may be shedding fat, but he's no longer shedding pounds as quickly as he did at first. Fat is much lighter than glucose and water, so he's hardly lost any more weight. To lose seven pounds of fat would take George another month.

George's willpower breaks. Frustrated by his slow weight loss and disappointed by a romance that won't get off the ground, he can no longer hold back his hunger drives. He orders a pizza—a super deluxe pizza, with extra cheese and double pepperoni. Then he orders another. Every mouthful brings George pure pleasure, a reward for answering his body's cry for energy.

Like most diets, George's full frontal assault on his fat stores has failed. But his friend Samson urges him to try a different tactic.

Top: Frustrated and disappointed, George caves in and eats two deluxe pizzas.

Bottom: Samson, George's friend, convinces him to try the gym.

WORKING OFF THE WEIGHT

So far George has turned down all opportunities for exercise. Now he decides to give it a try, and he heads for the gym. But when it comes to losing weight there's no such thing as a free lunch. After years of neglect his muscles aren't prepared for what's about to happen.

Top: George begins his workout at the gym, but at an unknown risk.

Bottom: After years without exercise, George's muscles are not prepared for the workout.

The blood supply to his muscle fibers has withered with disuse, so very little fuel can be delivered to them. Inside every muscle cell are emergency stores of fast-burning glucose. But these provide just a short burst of energy. As George works out, his energy demands soar. His muscles need to generate 50 times more energy than normal. His mitochondria don't have a hope of meeting the demand. The task is simply overwhelming.

The effort exhausts George, who feels that his sudden bout of exercise has done him more

Top: The weak blood supply of George's muscle fibers provides little energy.

Bottom: The workout requires more energy than George's mitochondria can supply.

harm than good. But, as he rests, an astounding metamorphosis begins.

George's body starts to prepare itself for the next bout of exercise, so that it will be better equipped to cope with the muscles' demand for energy. Throughout his muscle fibers new blood vessels are growing, increasing supplies of blood and, with it, energy-rich fat. And deep within the muscle cells his mitochondria start to divide, doubling the energy they can generate.

Exercise is transforming George's body to burn more fat. And as his fuel demands

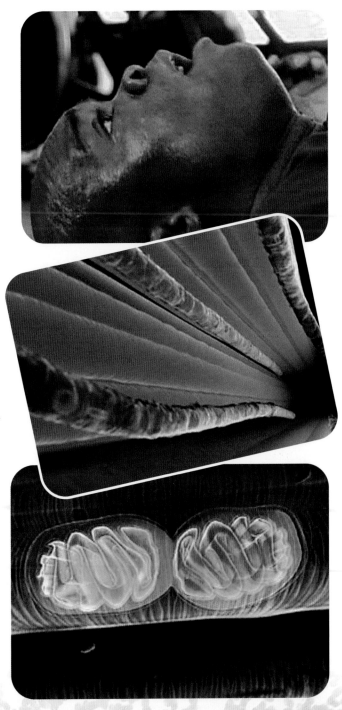

Top: George rests after his tough workout.

Middle and bottom: As George rests, his body increases its blood supply and his energy starts to flow.

rise, his fat depots release their stores. But because George isn't starving himself, this release of fat does not shock his body into thinking famine has arrived. His hunger drives are kept at bay.

It's a virtuous circle. The more George works out, the more efficient his muscles become at burning fat.

And the more fat they burn, the more energy he has. After eight weeks of vigorous exercise, they have become fat-burning machines. More fat is being delivered to the

Top: Exercise helps the body to burn more fat.

Middle: George starts to work out more and eat better, which helps his body to avoid hunger pangs.

Bottom: The body's fat stores release and begin to burn.

muscles, and there are now many more mitochondria to burn it.

The fat stores around George's gut begin to melt away. They're not just shrinking; they're also moving to where they are most needed. To ensure a constant supply of instant energy, muscle cells have begun to stockpile their own minireserves of fat.

Top: George's muscles now burn fat regularly and produce more mitochondria.

Bottom: The exercise routine has shrunk George's fat stores and created minireserves of energy.

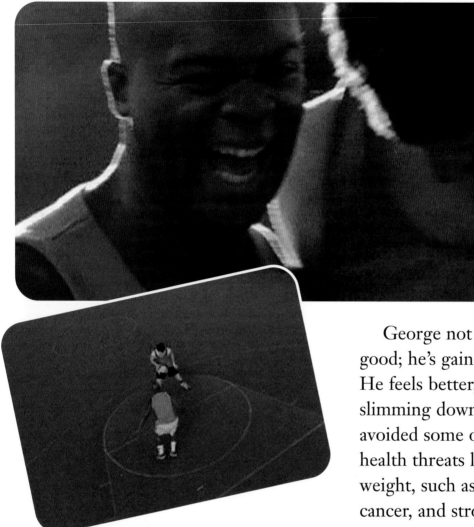

Top: Now that George has changed his eating and exercise habits, he looks better, has more energy, and exudes confidence.

Bottom: George must continue his new habits to keep his body healthy.

George not only looks good; he's gained confidence. He feels better, and by slimming down he may have avoided some of the serious health threats linked to excess weight, such as heart disease, cancer, and stroke. But the changes to his body aren't permanent. If he stops exercising and returns to overeating, they could go as quickly as they have come. Fat will always be just a few mouthfuls away.

GLOSSARY

bacteria Microscopic organisms, some of which cause disease

carbohydrates A major class of animal foods that includes sugars and starches

glucose A sugar that is used by the body as a speedy energy booster

immune system The system that protects the body from harmful foreign substances

intestines The tubular part of the digestive tract in which digestion is completed

lymph gland A round mass of lymphoid tissue; aids in cleaning the blood

macrophage A cell that helps to protect the body against disease

metamorphosis Transformation

mitochondria Structures in cells that produce energy for the body

molecule The smallest particle of a substance that retains the chemical and physical properties of the substance

protein An essential part of animal foods that includes meat, fish, eggs, and milk

salmonella A type of bacteria that is harmful to humans and other mammals

villi Fingerlike projections in the stomach that absorb water and nutrients

INDEX